REESE

To Mrs. Landenberger & the Second Grade Class

Nancy Meyer

Pauline Cox

Written by
**Pauline Cox &
Nancy Meyer**

Photographed by
Nancy Meyer

To order additional copies of this book, contact:
Xlibris Corporation
1-888-795-4274
www.Xlibris.com
Orders@Xlibris.com

Reese is a Sumatran orangutan who lives in the ABQ BioPark with her parents Sarah and Tonka.

She was born October 2, 2008 and like all youngsters, she loves to explore. At times, her dad has to come to her rescue especially when her hands slip on a bar and she needs his help to keep her from falling by easing her to the ground.

Her antics and facial expressions are so precious that this book had to be written.

With special thanks to:

Abq Biopark of Albuquerque, N.M.

Kristen Aguilar for transcribing this book.

Now, Reese, you listen to your Mama.

Mama I wuv you.

I need a hug.

Rock-a-by-baby!

Daddy, Daddy, look at me – look at me.

Look Ma – No hands!

What's this Mom? Huh? Huh?

Wonder what's under here?

Hello up there

Dad, Dad wake up!

Aw Daddy, I won't fall

Whoops!

Oh, no!

Daddy! Help!

Thanks, Dad!

I'm hungry

HUH ?

Ooh, broccoli!

I like this

Snacktime

This looks good – must be salad.

Come on – I'm not afraid of you.

Are they gone?

Mom — I need a comb.

Bet'cha you can't do this.

Peek-A-Boo

What can I get into next?

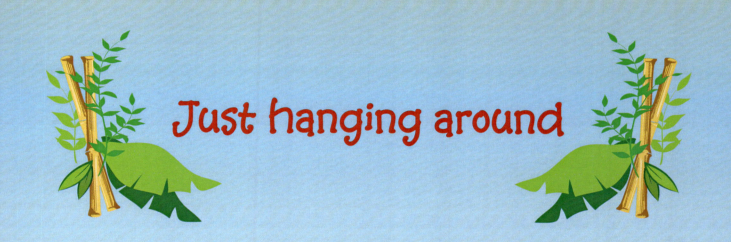

Just hanging around

I hope you come to Albuquerque to see me.

So I can see you.